A New Cartridge
The 480 Achilles

By Jim Taylor with Lewis Ballard, Aaron Bittner, Doug Mann and John Killebrew

During it's lifetime the Colt Single Action Army was produced in a wonderful variety of calibers. Most people are familiar with the .45 Colt as well as some of other more famous cartridges it was chambered for. While the .45 Colt, the .44-40, the .32-20 and others are pretty well known, not very many people are familiar with the largest caliber it was made in, the .476 Eley.

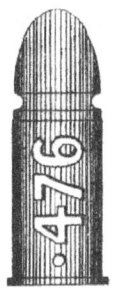
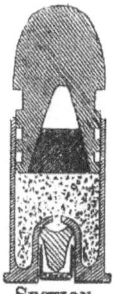

SECTION.

A mysterious cartridge, it is hard for the average sixgunphyle to find out much written about it. "Cartridges of the World" has some data for the .476 Eley Mark II and Mark III but even there the details are sketchy and leave many unanswered questions. For instance, what was the actual barrel diameter of the Colt's pistol in that caliber? What did the chambers look like? Were they bored straight through like the .41 Long Colt or what?

We know the cartridge itself was a British military round and that it was used for only a few years. The Mark II and Mark III variation apparently could also be fired in the .455 Eley, meaning that if the .476 Eley actually had a .476" diameter bore, the bullet was undersized, at least in the later "Marks". I have read that the .476 Eley used a .472" diameter bullet .. which just adds to the confusion. "Cartridges of the World" says the .476 Eley Mark III used a hollow-based bullet with a clay plug in the base of the bullet to get it to expand to bore diameter. That it was less than satisfactory would probably be an understatement.

Dave Scovill in his excellent book "Loading the Peacemaker - Colt's Model P" (Wolfe Publishing Co., 6471 Airpark Dr., Prescott, AZ 86301) says on pages 18 and 19 that the .476 Eley was similar to the .455 Colt cartridge. He says it "..featured a 288 gr. .454-inch bullet over 18 grains of blackpowder.......A clay plug in the hollow base bullet caused it to expand to fit the barrel." So a quick search shows some conflicting statements between authors, at least on the surface.

Not content with what I had found, I kept searching and finally turned up a book entitled "Colt Peacemaker Revolver Caliber .476 Eley " - a book devoted entirely to the round and the Colt's revolvers produced in that caliber! I ordered one immediately. Written by Keith Cochran and published by "Cochran Publishing Co." in Rapid City, SD this 55 page book contains more information about the 476 Eley than I knew existed, information about the guns that I could find no place else.

In this book Mr. Cochran says that some .476 Eley ammunition featured a *"....straight lead bullet with one grease groove outside the cartridge case ..."* These, he says, will not chamber in the ..455 Eley, whereas the later .476 Eley does in fact chamber in the .455 Eley.

I surmise from his writings that the first .476 Eley's featured a heeled bullet, though it's hard to tell for sure. It could be that the bullet was just too long for the .455 chamber. Whatever the bullet was, the British Army apparently did not want the supply problems of two different calibers and so their solution was to make all the ammo fit all the pistols! Thus the .45 caliber bullet with the clay plug to force it to fit the large .476 Eley bore but still shoot just fine in the .455 Eley.

Mr. Cochran's data on the .476 Eley shows a bullet weight of 270 gr. for the later variations of the cartridge. (He says the earlier heavier bullet would not chamber in the .455 Eley, as I stated above.) He shows the bore diameter of the .476 Eley as .476" - .477".

To say that there has been very little excitement over the .476 Eley would be over-stating the situation by a lot. It is a dead cartridge except to certain collectors, historians, and those who love to dabble in the weird and forgotten of the shooting world. Which brings us to the theme of this article ... the 480 Achilles.

A Giant Step Backward?

The 480 Achilles is the product of 5 slightly warped minds, Lewis Ballard, Aaron Bittner, John Killebrew, Doug Mann and me, Jim Taylor. The project was a collaborative effort upon which we pooled our brains. The puddle which resulted from this pooling may have been shallow but at least it was slippery.

Lewis Ballard speaks:

One day I decided that what the world really needed was a new, big bore revolver cartridge. Now there are plenty of fine big bore revolver cartridges out there already. Used to be I could just say, "Pick any cartridge that starts with a .4 and we'll have a fine big bore revolver cartridge," but that doesn't work anymore, especially now that we've got the various .50s (the .50 AE, .500 Linebaugh, .500 Linebaugh Long, .500 Smith and Wesson, .50 Special, and probably some others I don't know about). Still, none of them really offered exactly what I wanted and besides, improvisation is lots of fun and keeps me off the streets.

I have always liked big bore, moderate power cartridges. The cartridge I've shot most consistently over the years is the .45

ACP and I remain entirely happy with it's type of ballistics, a 230 grain bullet at about 850 feet per second. Whether in a 1911, a double action revolver (several Smith and Wesson 1917s over the years) or a single action revolver the .45 ACP is easy and fun to shoot, giving simple big bore performance. Inspired by the .45 ACP I wondered what kind of big bore cartridge could be cooked up that would perform similarly.

There are mild big bore loadings available today. Buffalo Bore Ammunition offers a .475 Linebaugh load with a 420 grain LFN at 950 feet per second and handloaders can come up with equivalent loads for the big bore cartridges. However, to take advantage of these you need a sixgun to shoot them through. The problem is, since these are subloads, the sixguns that shoot them have to be capable of taking the full charge versions of these cartridges. The situation is equivalent to shooting SAAMI-spec .44 Special loads through a .44 Magnum sixgun. There's just more steel there than the load really calls for. At this point in my musings I was distracted by, if I remember correctly, a Martini .22 target rifle. They say that one of the benefits of a liberal arts education is the ability to make connections between seemingly unrelated incidents or things. Well, as I looked at the Martini I realized that the most common cartridge in America (if not the world) might hold the answer to my predicament: the .22 Long Rifle. The .22 LR is both ubiquitous and unusual in that it is both a rimfire cartridge and it uses a "heeled" bullet.

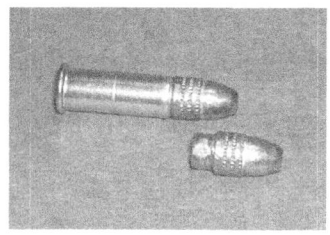

While most modern cartridges use a bore-diameter bullet that fits inside the case with the case being larger than bore size, heeled bullet cartridges use a two-diameter bullet with the shank smaller than bore diameter and fitting inside a case which matches bore size. The .45 Colt at the case mouth measures .480". Would it be possible to come up with a heeled bullet of .475" to fit into a .45 Colt case for use in a sixgun fitted with a .475" barrel and a bored-through cylinder? (The cylinder would have no chamber "step") If so, a sixgun of Colt SAA dimensions could be used as a base gun since the SAA is already available in the .45 Colt case.

I couldn't think of any reason it wouldn't work. This in and of itself doesn't mean much. I am an idea man. But translating my goofy ideas into reality is one of the reasons that there are gunsmiths out there. I chewed the idea over with Doug Mann, Aaron Bittner and John Killebrew and they didn't see any reason it couldn't work. So I got in touch with Jim Taylor. I figured if anyone could discourage me in my madness it would be Jim Taylor. To my infinite shock and delight it turned out that he'd had the same idea a couple of years previously. (This happens all the time: look at the .244 Remington, which recreated a light bullet load of the old 6x57mm Mauser.)

The basic idea was to create a heeled, big bore bullet at roughly .45 ACP hardball velocity, more or less 850 feet per second. With the basic idea enunciated I became more or less useless, sitting on the sidelines and enthusiastically applauding the bullet design, case design and ballistic calculations that were carried out by Doug, Aaron, John and Jim.

Jim Taylor speaks again:

What is interesting is that I had the same idea as Lewis Ballard. I spoke with Hamilton Bowen about the feasibility of building the gun and cartridge 3 or 4 years ago. When Lewis contacted me about the project and asked if I wanted to be a part there was no hesitation! This is something I had been wanting to do.

Doug Mann speaks about his part of the project:

My initial involvement in the project came as a sounding board for Lewis - that is, whenever he gets one of these squirrelly ideas, he bounces them off me so that I can tell him he's nuts.

Well we started that way, but the more I pondered it the more I thought - why not?

From that point - i.e., accepting that it could be done, Lewis involved Aaron and John - Aaron for his experience in bullet design and working with Dan at Mountain Molds, and John because, well because he knows a lot and can do a lot and after all, he is the Teddy Bear of Death.

Heeled bullets are nothing new - indeed

they are a throwback to the early days of metallic cartridges. Many of the first cartridge designs used heeled bullets. The early .44 Colt and more notably Colt's .41 Long Colt enjoyed some success, and the oldest heeled design of all, the .22 rimfire cartridge, is still going strong. Yet, no one has designed a heeled bullet cartridge in the 21st Century - until now.

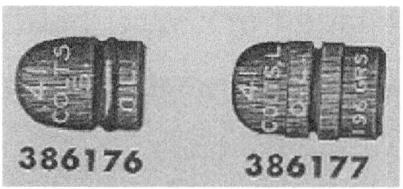
.41 Colt Heel Bullets

Over the next few weeks, the four of us at various times - and with all this being done via the Internet - kicked this idea just about to death. We went from using .45 Schofield brass to .45 Auto Rim brass and ultimately decided on cut down .45 Colt brass because: 1) it is plentiful and relatively cheap; and 2) once trimmed to .900, the resulting case mouth is fairly thick and should crimp down fairly tight on the heel.

This all being done, there was a need for legitimization - i.e., a respected member of the media or firearms industry or at least somebody who knew somebody, so Lewis suggested we snooker Jim into this cabal. Mainly because we knew he'd try anything once. Also we needed a name and literary/artistic input.

So my main role has been to encourage the others to do their best work by telling them what wouldn't work or pointing out flaws or fuzzy thinking.

Jim Taylor's Perspective on the new caliber:

First and foremost, there exists no need for this caliber. Other than being unique it is totally without merit. Thus our motto:

Undaunted by common sense

Second, the idea was (in my mind at least) to create a modern version of the 476 Eley. A heavy big-bore bullet at low velocity.

Third, we wanted to do this in a way that was as simple as possible.

Designing the cartridge

Between us we came up with the idea of boring the .45 Colt chamber straight through (like a .22 Long Rifle chamber) and using a "heel" bullet as has been stated. Since the outside of the .45 Colt is not to much larger than .475" this would put us right at the diameter of the bullet we wanted.

Looking through a standard chamber you can see the "step".

Comparison Of Chamber Types

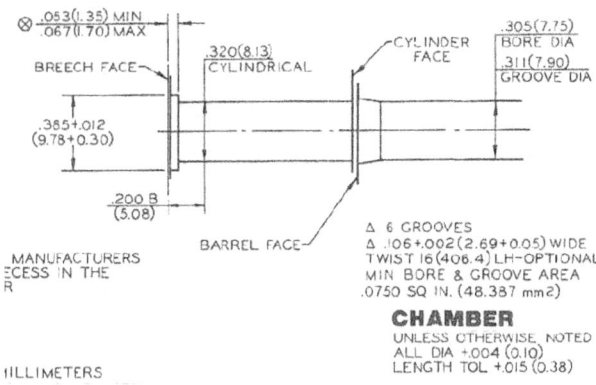

.32 Short Colt

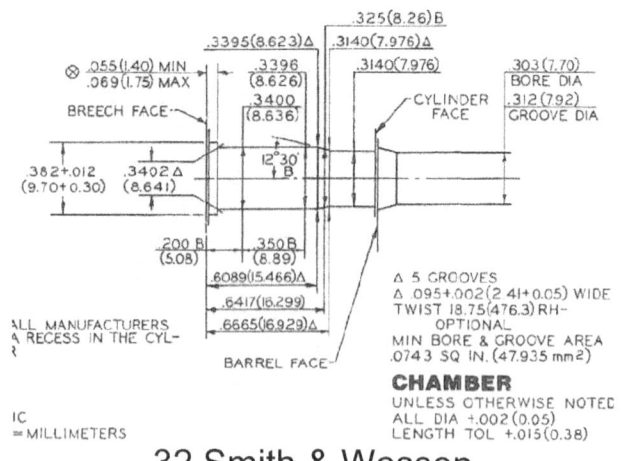

32 Smith & Wesson

Straight-through chamber

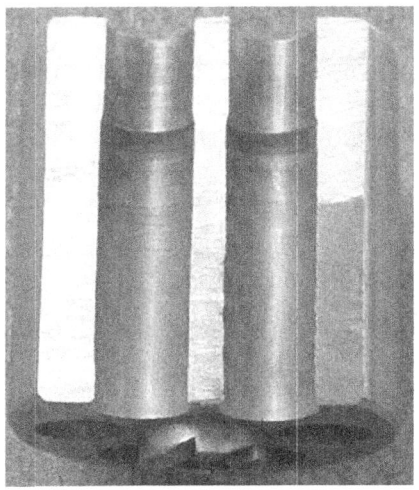
"Stepped" chamber

Note the step where it goes from cartridge diameter to bullet diameter.

Aaron Bittner set about designing the bullet and contacting the mold-maker. He had a contact at Mountain Molds. Mountain Molds has online mold designing software so you can design your own bullet. Discussions about the length of the heel were ongoing as Aaron kept working on the bullet design. My suggestion was to keep the proportions (bullet body to heel ratio) at close to what the .22 Long Rifle 40 gr. bullet has.

Aaron Bittner speaks On Designing the Bullet for 480 Achilles

When I first heard about Lewis's idea for the .480 Achilles I was intrigued. Think about it: A true .475 revolver cartridge that fits in the standard six-shot SAA (or any other .45-caliber revolver, for that matter) without any need for scratch-built cylinders or supplemental life insurance. The idea seemed a winner.

The key to the Achilles' success was to be a bullet that occupied the full width of the outside of the cartridge case — .476 in the case of the .45 ACP and .45 Colt. It was a happy coincidence that .475 is already a standard bore size. But the success of the cartridge would depend, in large part, on how well the bullet worked.

Designing a bullet is a little like designing an airplane in that it's an exercise in trade-offs. If you want a better ballistic coefficient, you have to give up some meplat; if you want better sectional density, you have to put up with more weight. In the case of the 480 Achilles there was an additional factor that I would have to account for: the heel, that part of the bullet that extends into the cartridge case.

At first I thought the of the presence of the heel as a real handicap. Heeled bullets require outside lubrication which tends to attract dust and dirt. A heel also reduces bearing surface on the bullet for a given weight. Heeled bullets require special tooling to crimp. Nevertheless heeled bullets have been used successfully for over a century; witness the humble (and hugely successful) .22 Long Rifle.

I started by making a list of the requirements for the cartridge itself. It would use a .475-caliber heeled bullet at low velocity utilizing a cartridge case of about the volume of a .45 ACP. I began to think of it as "like a .45 Auto, only more so." (It seemed better than imagining that we were re-inventing the .476 Eley.) To maximize the effectiveness of the cartridge it should use a soft lead bullet with a wide, flat striking surface. The proposed pressure levels were low (around standard ACP levels or 16,000 psi) so it could use a soft alloy. I also wanted it heavier than .45 ACP ball. And of course it would need that heel.

The first consideration was bullet weight. It would be over 230 grains at least. The need for a heel added to bullet weight without contributing to bearing surface, so everything forward of the case mouth would have to earn its keep. Bearing surface would be at a premium so on the strength of TLAR theory (That Looks About Right) I figured on 325 grains for an upper limit. This would later be pared back to 300 grains as we hedged our bets.

Remember when I said that designing bullets was an exercise in trade-offs? This time I found a win-win in the choice of profile. I thought it a good idea to maximize the bullet's bearing surface...but I also like a bullet with a big flat nose (meplat). Bearing surface and meplat happen to go together real well.

The next step was to go to the Mountain Molds website and start fiddling around with Dan's online bullet design program. Because Dan's program doesn't have an option for a heel, I specified a long gas-check shank. I started fiddling with options and having the program draw the bullets. Here are some of the early results. Some of these are heavier than our final spec:

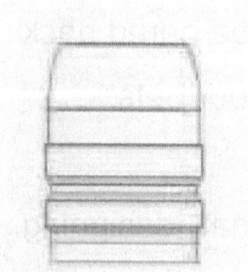 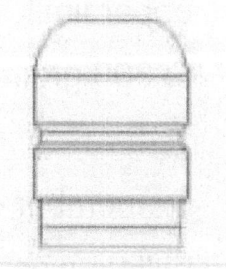

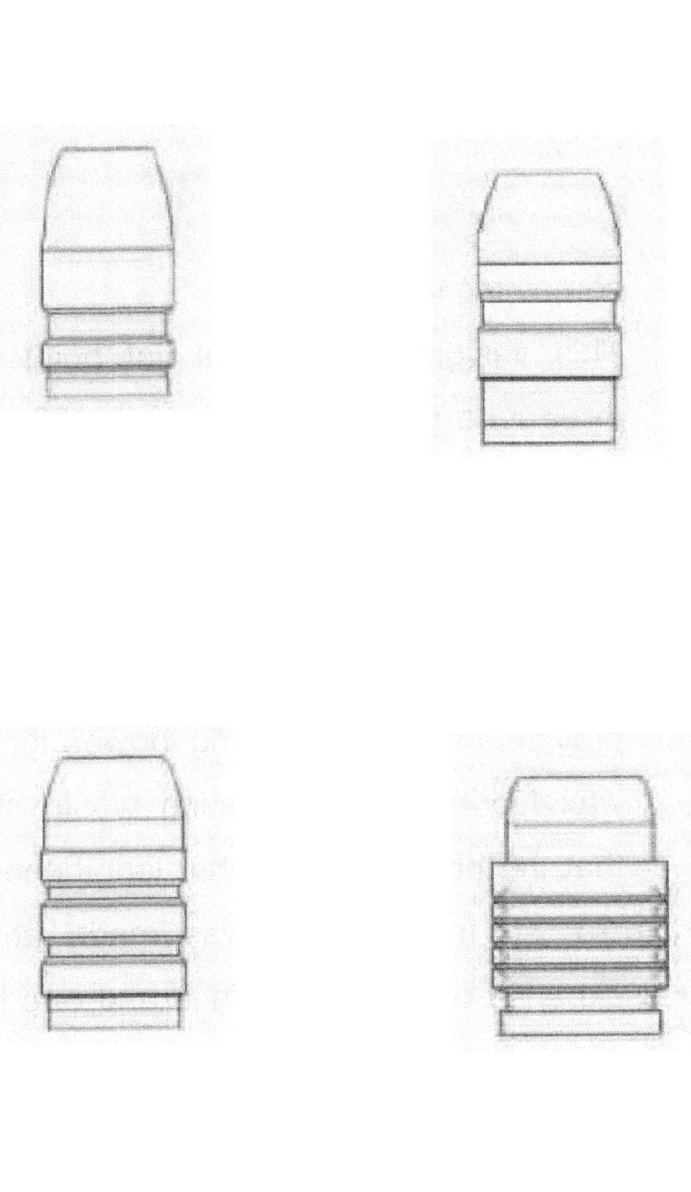

In the end the design that won out was

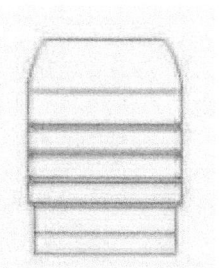

something very like this:

This design is an ogival flat point with three lube grooves and a heel .150 long. The meplat is 80 percent of the bullet diameter. The bullet would weigh 300 grains when cast of 20:1 alloy. The three fine lube grooves are there to try to provide maximum holding power for dry wax lubricant. Later testing would show that the heel worked better lengthened to .20, so that change was made at the expense of bearing surface and one lube groove. This is the final version -

Ultimately the 480 Achilles is a limited round shooting a limited bullet...but within those limits I have high hopes. Perhaps the design is funny-looking. I'm going to withhold judgment until we see how it flies.

Jim Taylor speaks again:

John Killebrew used the QuickLoad program to run some computer tests and define what the bullet weight/powder charge/performance parameters would be. We figured on a 300 gr. bullet at moderate velocity, since the original 476 Eley used a

288 gr. bullet at moderate velocity. What John came up with was an optimum case length of .90". This figured right into our plans, since the .476 Eley used a .88" case length.

QUICKLOAD DATA FOR THE 480 Achilles
300gr heeled bullet in all loads, 7.5" barrel

NOTE: THIS IS NOT DATA FROM TEST FIRING. IT IS COMPUTER-GENERATED DATA DESIGNED TO HELP US LEARN WHERE TO START TESTING.

This data was developed for the first version of the bullet which had a heel only .130" in length instead of the .200" that the final version of the bullet has. This data is approximately 7% off ... BUT it did give us a good starting point.

6.0grs / 34% fill / 14Kpsi / 829fps

Bullseye:

5.5grs / 40% fill / 13Kpsi / 840fps

6.0grs / 44% fill / 15Kpsi / 891fps

Unique:

6grs / 52% fill / 12Kpsi / 825fps

6.5grs / 56% fill / 13Kpsi / 872fps

7grs / 60% fill / 15Kpsi / 920fps

2400:

11.0grs / 58% fill / 9.0Kpsi / 806fps

12.0grs / 63% fill / 11Kpsi / 877fps

The data generated by QuickLoad gave us a good idea of where to start testing. I decided my first loads would be with Unique. The reason I decided on Unique is that it is not as "fast" a powder as Bullseye or 231 and it filled the case decently. My experience with 2400 led me to want to wait until other loads had been developed.

I settled on 5.0 gr. of Unique as a good starting place. I would work up loads gradually, chronographing them to keep track of everything.

Naming the baby

During this time a name for cartridge was being tossed around. Eventually we settled on "480 Achilles". "Achilles" because of the heel obviously. "480" was chosen because that's the way it popped out. And it stuck.

During all this deep and heavy brain work Gary Reeder of Reeder Custom Guns (www.reedercustomguns.com) was contacted to see if he would be interested in building the guns for us. After some discussion he agreed and ordered the reamers for the re-chambering from Dave Manson of Manson Reamers (http://www.mansonreamers.com), Since Gary Reeder builds .475 caliber guns we knew he would have barrel stock on hand. And he seemed slightly intrigued by the idea. I mean, at least he wasn't noticeably yawning on the phone while I rattled on and on about this new cartridge.

The First Gun

Looking around for a suitable gun to build the 480 Achilles on I had several criteria in mind. I wanted it to be on the Colt SAA-size frame and I did not want to pay "new gun" prices for a gun that was going to be completely remodeled. At least not if I didn't have to.

I could have easily gone with a used Ruger Blackhawk. The Ruger single actions have a much stronger frame, better springs and are very suitable for customizing. However, I wanted to keep my gun at least somewhat on the lines of the old Colt since we were "re-creating" an old Colt cartridge (at least my mind). After a few days a friend contacted me that he had a gun for me that would work for this project, a "Cabela's Millennium" revolver in .45 Colt. These are the cheaper version of the Colt SAA put out by Uberti for Cabela's. The interiors of the guns are identical to the other versions, but the finish is basically just sand-blasted (or "bead-blasted') and looks more like Parkerizing than bluing. The backstrap and trigger guard are of brass instead of steel.

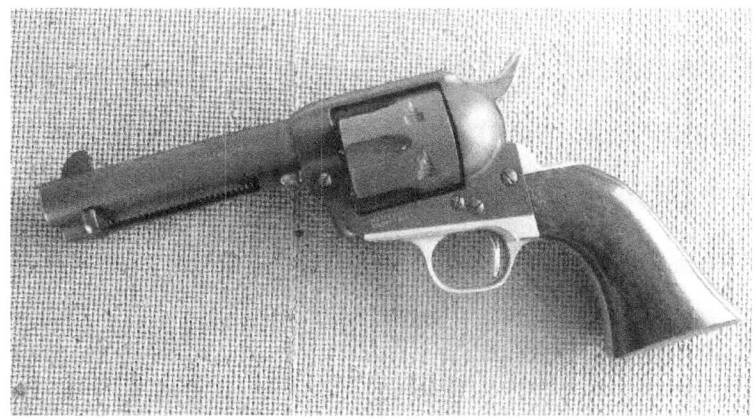

When I picked up the gun I decided to

shoot it a bit and almost did not go through with using it to make the 480 Achilles! The gun functioned perfectly and was smooth and accurate. Shooting some of my .45 Colt Cowboy loads I was able to keep my shots on a rock about the size of my hat at a distance of nearly 100 yards! I used it in a Cowboy Action match and the gun functioned perfectly. It felt right at home in my hand ... and I had twinges about remodeling it.

However once I had it in the shop at home I got back on track. Pulling the gun apart I removed all the "safety" features in the hammer. On the "new" gun they would not be wanted. I also installed a new cylinder bushing and a Belt Mountain base pin. Once I had that done I packaged it up and sent it off to Reeder Custom Guns.

I had wanted to replace the brass backstrap and trigger guard with a steel one. I asked a few friends and John Taffin was kind enough to furnish a Colt backstrap and trigger guard. I included these with the gun when I sent it off to Reeder Custom Guns, along with instructions as to barrel length, grips, finish, sights, etc.

Ammunition

While Mr. Reeder was working on the gun, we went to work trying to get some ammo to him so that he could test-fire it as it was being finished. The bullet molds were not yet done so John Killebrew took a day and turned some 440 gr. .500 Linebaugh bullets into 300 gr. 480 Achilles bullets on his lathe. A slow, time-consuming process, it never-the-less gave us the first bullets for test purposes.

While John was making the bullets I prepared the cartridge cases. I used .45 Colt cases that had neck splits or cracks. With a drill attached to it I used my RCBS Case Trimmer to cut them to length. The cases were then deburred, chamfered, sized, deprimed, primed and then set aside to await the arrival of the bullets. When I received John's home-made bullets I loaded 10 rounds to send to Gary Reeder. 5 were loaded with 18 gr. of DuPont FFg black powder, and 5 were loaded with 5.0 gr. of Unique.

I bell-mouthed the cartridge cases using an RCBS expander plug that I ground to taper. I use this on my 454's and .45 Colt loads. I expanded the neck just enough so that the bullet heel would start into the case. The bullets were then seated to the correct depth.

After seating all the bullets I ran the loaded rounds into a 454 carbide sizing die. The die is a pretty tight one and I wanted to "mash" the bell-mouth back against the heel of the bullet, since I did not have a crimping die yet. Doing it this way seemed to work OK.

The final step was to lube the bullets. I rubbed some Apache Blue lube into the grease grooves by hand, then applied a light coat of Lee Liquid Alox to "bond" it all together.

Loading Dies

One of the things we needed was a crimp die. We figured the easiest way to make a crimp die would be the "collett-type" dies that Lee Precision makes. John Killebrew contacted Lee Precision and talked to them and they said they couldn't make one for us. Something about the cartridge body being too short or some such thing. That only made the engineer in John set up and say, "Hey, what do mean?" and he decided to work on one himself.

In the meantime I contacted Kelye

Schlepp of Belt Mountain Enterprises (the Belt Mountain base pin guy www.beltmountain.com) and asked him about a crimping device. When I explained what the cartridge and bullet was he said there were some colletts used in machining that might work and that he would get on it! Cool. Two heads working on a project are better than one.

As far as the rest of the loading process, the empties can be resized and depimed in standard .45 Colt dies. The necks can be expanded with normal dies available or a person can make one like I use. Priming is standard .45 Colt. Bullet seating can be done with .45 Colt dies by running the seating plug quite a ways out toward the base. All that is needed is the proper nose shape on the end to keep from deforming the bullet. So you can see the crimping die is THE die that we needed.

The crimp is essential to keep the loaded round from "pooping". By that I mean that without a crimp it is quite possible for the bullet to be moved from the cartridge by the force of the primer before the powder charge has ignited. Proper pressures will not be developed, nor will they be consistent, all detrimental to accuracy. With a heeled bullet like the 480 Achilles it is all the more critical since you have the major portion of the bullet outside of the cartridge case. Thus the cartridge itself does not help much in the way of adding to the force required to get the bullet moving .. "bullet pull" in technical terms.

Test-firing the Prototype

Gary Reeder called me in the middle of all this to say that the gun was "coming together" and that they had test-fired it with the cobbled-up ammo I had sent. Since it did not have a crimp he only loaded one cartridge at a time, but said the gun worked just fine and all the shots went "...into a small cluster at the bottom of the black at 15 yards..." We agreed that it would be best to leave the front sight extra high so that it could be regulated with the correct ammo once we had all the dies. Mr. Reeder said the gun was going back to the shop for finish work and to have a set of grips fabricated. After discussion we agreed upon a set of Mesquite grips for it. This was getting exciting!

Bullet Mold

The bullet mold arrived at John Killebrew's around this time and he began to cast some bullets and take photos of them for us. The bullet weighed right at 290 gr. which was a target weight for us. The main body is .477" and the heel is .455". John cast a bunch of bullets and then sent the mold to me. As soon as I got it fired up my lead pot and made about 200 from pure lead. My plan was to make some of pure lead, some of 50/50 pure lead and wheel weights and some of straight wheel weights to see if there would be any accuracy difference.

After weighing and measuring the bullets I christened the mold the "Bittner 480-290-FNH". The specs on the bullets are:

Bittner-480-290-FNH

Weight: 290 gr. (wheelweights & 2% tin)

292 gr. (pure lead)

Length: .634"

Body diameter: .4778"

Meplat to heel: .435"

Meplat: .388"

Heel diameter: .455"

Silk Purse Out Of A Sow's Ear

While experiments were still on-going in the efforts to develop a proper crimp die Gary Reeder called and said the gun was finished and that he was shipping it back. The next few days I was on pins and needles waiting for it to arrive. I don't usually get this anxious but I was excited about getting my hands on this gun.

One Tuesday as I was on the shooting range I noticed the UPS truck coming my way. I went to the gate to meet him and he said he had a package for me! He also said that when he found I was not at home he figured I would be on the range. Love that brown truck! I took the package, opened it up and found a completely new gun! I had sent a Millennium revolver to Reeder and I got back what looked like a custom Colt SAA! It was beautiful. And it did not bear any resemblance to the gun I

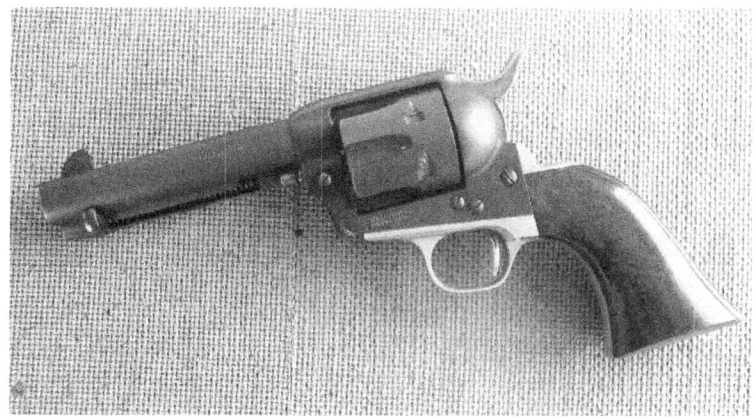

had sent off!

Before

After

The gun had a 7 1/2" barrel with a custom front sight. The grips were of Mesquite and nicely finished. If you look closely at the photo of the grips you can see the worm holes Mesquite is famous for. Reeder had fitted the Colt SAA backstrap and trigger guard and mated them perfectly. There was enough engraving on the gun to really set off the deep black

finish. On the left side of the

barrel it was marked "480 ACHILLES" ... on the top were the names of all the team that worked on it .. BALLARD - BITTNER - KILLEBREW - MANN - TAYLOR. The right side of the barrel was marked PROTOTYPE in gold lettering.

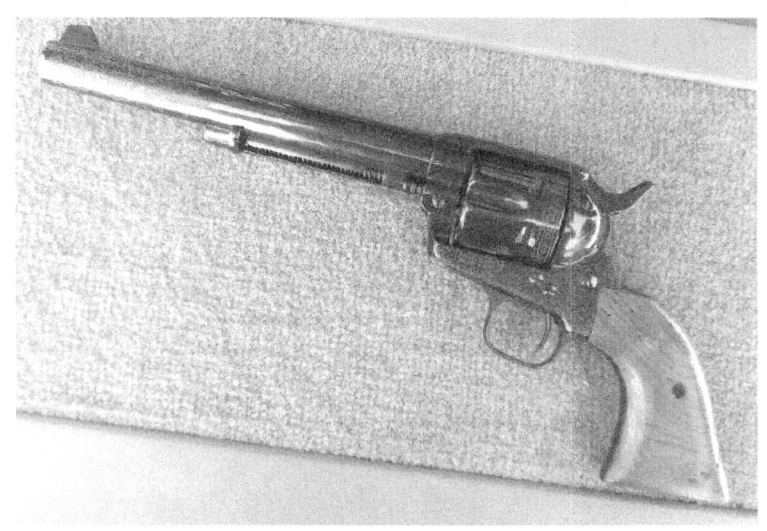

I immediately went to the shop and grabbed about 30 rounds of ammo I previously loaded. On the range I fired the first shots and found the gun to be extremely pleasant to shoot. A big thumper, recoil was very mild. Reeder had the sights centered and I found it easy to hit hedge apples (about the size of a softball) at 25 yards offhand.

I did not do any testing at this time. I was just enjoying shooting the gun too much.

That would wait for a later day. Right now was a time to bask in the enjoyment of a plan coming together. Whether the accuracy would prove to be adequate later on or not, for just plain fun this gun was a blast!

Reeder had indeed taken a "sow's ear" and turned it into a "silk purse". This gun looked good and shot well with our home-built ammo.

Making Ammo That Works

While the crimp die was not yet operational I had come up with an alternative that would get by for a time. At least I hoped it would.

Using a .45-70 Lee Factory Crimp collett-type die I had figured out that if I inserted a loaded 480 Achilles round into the die until the case neck was even with the end of the crimping portion of the die, and if I had a "spacer" of the correct length, I could crimp the 480 Achilles rounds with the .45-70 Lee die! I trimmed a .45 Colt cartridge until it was the correct length for a "spacer" and started loading some test ammo. It made a funky-looking almost-necked down cartridge BUT the crimp held!

I had picked Harry O's brain for as much information about the heel bullets as I could get. One thing he was adamant about - CRIMP IS IMPORTANT with heel bullets. So .. we had a way to crimp them until a regular crimp die was produced. Initial loadings were light. Since I really had no idea how the ammo would work I stated out very light. So light in fact that the cartridges were not sealing in the chamber and got very smoky. But I would rather be safe than sorry. Our plan was to work up slowly using the chronograph. My thoughts were that if we could get an honest 825 to 850 fps without causing undue strain on the gun we would have quite thumper!

I had been making the Achilles brass by taking my cracked .45 Colt cases and cutting them down to .90" length. The cases had cracked because of becoming brittle due to sizing, shooting, sizing, shooting etc. These cases sometimes tended to crack again when fired in the 480 Achilles. In the first 4 rounds fired I had one split full length. To remedy that problem I began annealing all the cases by heating the case mouth a dull red and dropping them in water. Anyone using previously cracked cases might consider annealing before loading the 480 Achilles.

Initial Testing

It was a windy day and I was pushed for time but I wanted to get the chronographing started so I headed to the range. The first loads I ran through the gun I knew would be light but they actually produced more than I thought they would averaging near 800 fps!

I ran 2 different loads of Unique and one load of 231 through the chronograph, then fired 3 rounds on a target at 25 yards. The groups was 2 1/2" low and bit to the left, falling into a triangle 1 3/4" center to center. I was out of ammo! If I had not had a busy day scheduled I would have loaded more, but it would have to wait.

RESULTS FOR THE DAY

All loads with the Bittner 480-290-FNH lubed with Lee Liquid Alox Tumble Lube
All with CCI Large Pistol Primers
All powder charges weighed

Powder & Charge	Average Velocity
231 - 6.0 gr.	794 fps
Unique - 6.1 gr.	798 fps
Unique - 6.5 gr.	848 fps

These were encouraging and showed that Quick Load was in the ball park. I ran out of ammo during the chronographing, but saved 3 rounds to shoot a target at 25 yards.

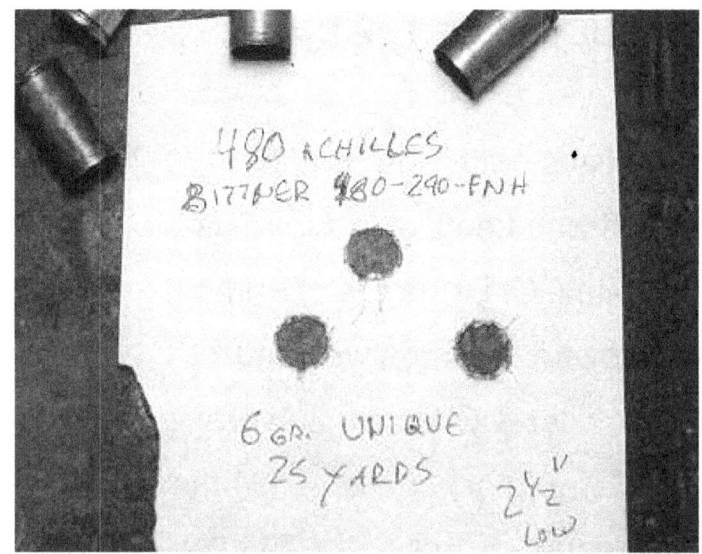

The first target - 25 yards - 1 3/4" center to center

From the first day of testing some recovered bullets.

More testing was In order but this was a good start! I found that shooting the 480 Achilles was a hoot and couldn't wait to get more ammo loaded.

Ongoing

Testing is ongoing as I write this. We do not know for sure yet how accurate this bullet is. There just is not a lot of information about heel bullets and we are feeling our way along. The crimp die that we need for a proper crimp is not yet finished. But we have a good start with what we put together ourselves and it has given us an idea of it's potential.

This is not a "magnum" nor is it intended to be "magnumized". In the Colt-sized guns one could quickly get past the safe point should they try to hot-rod it. As stated at the first, our goal was a large bore bullet at moderate velocity. That we have achieved. Now we work on developing accurate loads. Somehow I have the feeling this will not be an easy path. We will keep folks updated as it goes on.

So far I have put about 100 rounds through the gun, mostly chronographing. It is very pleasant and mild to shoot. The report of the shots is not loud (yes we wear ear protection) and recoil is very mild. It is FUN to shoot and I am having a ball!

LAST

The name of the gun is "480 Achilles". Note that there is no "." in front of "480". This is not a caliber, just a name. We are in the process of copyrighting the name, not to keep folks from using it. We could not do that anyhow - not that we want to. Any gunsmith who builds one can put the name of the gun on the cartridge or gun without violating the copyright.

We are copyrighting it as a reminder to folks that we would like a surcharge of $20 from the purchaser of each gun to go into a Missions Fund to help Sixgunner Missionaries - such as Paul Moreland. Paul is an avid sixgunner and a great guy as well as a good friend. He can use all the help he can get and we hope by this idea to make folks aware of his work and in a small way, help him in his endeavors.

You can check Paul's work out at http://www.sacm.net Hopefully this will not only be a fun project, but a useful one also.

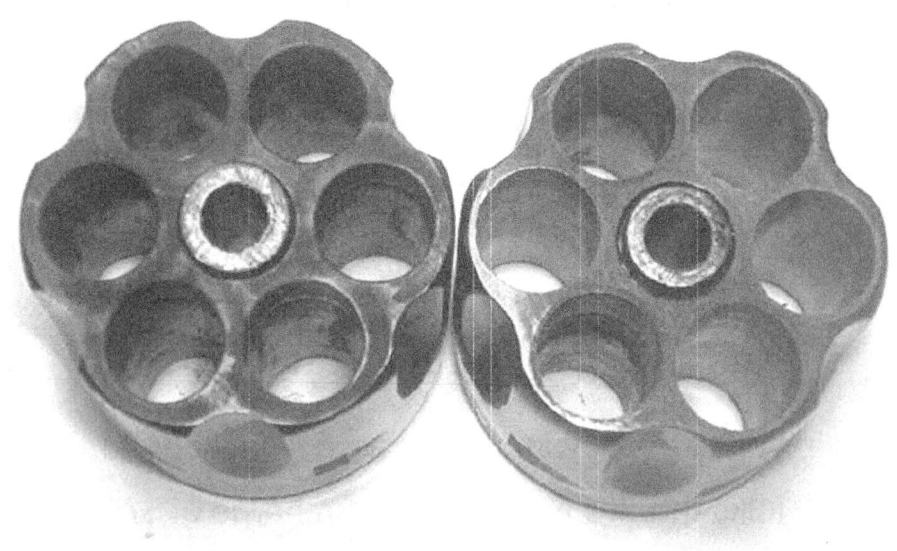

Left- 45 Colt cylinder
Right - 480 Achilles cylinder

480 ACHILLES LOAD DATA

All loads use CCI Large Pistol Primers

All loads with the Bittner 480-290-FNH bullet (290 gr. heel bullet)

All fired from 7 ½" barrel

7 feet from muzzle to first screen

All velocities are averages

Black Powder

- 21.0 gr. FFg DuPont - 643 fps (these were VERY consistent)

WW 231

- 6.0 gr. 231 = 794 fps

Bullseye

- 5.0 gr. Bullseye = 717 fps
- 6.0 gr. Bullseye = 883 fps

700X

- 6.0 gr. 700X = 906 fps

Unique

- 6.1 gr. Unique = 798 fps
- 6.5 gr. Unique = 848 fps
- 7.0 gr. Unique = 911 fps

2400

- 12.0 gr. 2400 = 870 fps (accurate load)
- 12.5 gr. 2400 = 885 fps
- 13.0 gr. 2400 = 950 fps (accurate load)

WC820 (military surplus H110)

- 15.5 gr. WC820 = 883 fps
- 16.0 gr. WC820 = 955 fps

This was written some years ago for the Leverguns.Com website and can still be found on there. In addition there are other articles about crimping experiments, making the brass, other types of bullets and some hunting that I have done with the 480 Achilles.

My thanks to everyone who was and who continues to be involved with this project. It was fun to do and is fun to play with. And no, it is not "better" than any other. It is just different. And it's ours.

Because we could.

Thanks to Lewis Ballard, Aaron Bittner, Doug Mann and John Killebrew without whose twisted minds this project would never have happened.

© Copyright 2004 Jim Taylor

Made in the USA
Coppell, TX
09 January 2024